# Lena Richard

The Creole Chef Who Redefined Southern Cooking and Built a Legacy in American Cuisine

Riley Anderson

Copyright © 2025 by Riley Anderson

Introduction..................................................................... 2

A Taste of New Orleans: The Early Years.................................. 4

Learning the Craft: From Local Kitchens to Culinary School 7

The Fannie Farmer Experience: Mastering the Art of Cooking 10

Coming Home with New Skills and Bigger Dreams.............. 13

Breaking Barriers in the Restaurant World............................16

The Cookbook That Made History........................................ 19

Cooking for the Airwaves: Radio and Television Stardom... 22

Teaching the Next Generation of Chefs................................. 25

Entrepreneurship on a Plate: From Catering to Frozen Foods. 28

A Legacy That Still Feeds the Soul...........................................31

Conclusion................................................................................34

# Introduction

There are lives that whisper and lives that sing. Lena Richard's life does both — a soft, steady hymn of craft and ambition that builds, note by note, into an unstoppable chorus. From a childhood threaded with Southern flavors to a professional career that put Creole cooking on radio, television, and dinner tables across America, Lena transformed ordinary ingredients into extraordinary opportunity. She taught herself techniques, invested in her skills, and dared to make business where others saw only limits. This book invites you to walk beside her: into kitchens warm with steam and pressure, into classrooms where recipes became careers, and into the tidy rows of a cookbook that would, unexpectedly, help rewrite a part of American culinary history.

Thank you for choosing to open this book. That choice matters. Reading biography is not a passive pastime — it is an act of attention that shapes what we value and whom we remember. By spending your time here, you are doing something powerful: you are rescuing a life from the margins and placing it where it belongs — in public view, subject to study and admiration. Lena's story rewards that attention. It is not only a chronicle of recipes and restaurants; it is a study in strategy, a manual for making opportunity out of craft, and a portrait of a woman who refused to accept the small roles society had prepared for her.

This introduction will take you only a few minutes, but the ideas it opens will stay with you. You will meet a woman who translated kitchen labor into vocational authority, who learned at the Fannie Farmer School and came home ready not merely to cook but to teach, to package, and to sell. You will see how radio and the newly arriving medium of television offered Lena a stage few Black women had then accessed — and how she turned that exposure into influence for students, customers, and aspiring professionals. You will follow a founder who launched a cooking school, ran restaurants, and even experimented with frozen prepared meals — ventures that speak to both daring and practicality.

As you read, watch for the patterns that made Lena effective. Notice how technical skill became a form of power; how documentation and reproducible methods turned oral tradition into teachable systems; and how entrepreneurship functioned as a tool for dignity in a segregated economy. Pay attention to the small pivots — a trip to a culinary school, a single successful menu, a cookbook sold door-to-door — because in Lena's life the modest decisions are where change begins.

I praise you now, sincerely and emphatically, for being the kind of reader who chooses to learn. Your engagement is essential: without readers who care to remember and to act, the work of people like Lena fades into footnotes. Your curiosity is the engine that keeps these stories alive. If Lena's life inspires you — to teach, to start a business, to insist on craftsmanship — then this book has done its job.

Turn the page. Learn how one woman's pots and pans became instruments of possibility, and how her recipes fed more than appetites — they fed a movement toward professional respect, financial independence, and cultural recognition. Your attention will make the difference.

# Chapter one

## A Taste of New Orleans: The Early Years

The first thing that greets you in Lena Richard's early world is not history but scent: the warm, fragrant welcome of a pot settling into its rhythm on a wood stove, the sweet-and-sour lift of caramelized onions, the slow, confident breathing of roux as it darkens to the color of well-wrewed tea. New Orleans taught Lena to read a kitchen the way other children learn to read letters. Markets, porches, and church suppers were classrooms where technique arrived through observation, repetition, and hands-on doing. In those neighborhoods, food was a language everyone spoke, and Lena listened with the kind of attention that later turned curiosity into craft.

She grew up amid a braided culinary culture—French, Spanish, African, Caribbean, and Native influences mixing in recipes passed down across generations. Families layered seasonings the way architects layer brick, mindful of balance and structure. Salt and spice were not arbitrary; they were tools for deepening memory. Lena's earliest lessons were practical: how heat transforms texture, how acids brighten a heavy dish, how a pinch can shift a flavor profile from ordinary to unforgettable. Those small, precise moves became the technical vocabulary that would later define her professional skill.

Community life accelerated her education. In New Orleans, home kitchens and neighborhood eateries operated as social hubs. Food marked rituals—baptisms, wakes, weddings—so cooks learned to produce both quantity and reliability. Lena watched women juggle vast pots and social expectations, and she learned that good cooking required not only talent but stamina and organization. She observed how menus were adjusted to seasons and celebrations, how leftover ingredients were reimagined, and how a seemingly simple plate could carry a family's reputation. Those lessons shaped her sense of culinary responsibility: cook well, feed many, and protect the dignity of the craft.

Markets were another school. Vendors displayed produce like scholars displaying knowledge—okra lined in tidy rows, okra velvet-smooth under the sun; citrus piled in pyramids, scent bursting with every touch. Lena learned to select ingredients by sight and touch, to judge ripeness with a fingertip. She saw how local availability shaped regional taste; what could be bought one week dictated what came to the table the next. That pragmatism—making great food from the season's honest offerings—became central to her approach. New Orleans cuisine in her hands would be both rooted and adaptable, proud of its origins yet practical in execution.

Family structure reinforced a craft-based ethic. Kitchens were shared spaces where multiple generations converged, and apprenticeship happened through proximity. A grandmother's instruction about simmer times sat beside a cousin's trick for seasoning birds; no one lesson stood alone. Lena absorbed this mosaic of knowledge and began to rehearse it. She practiced the measured patience necessary for long stews, the vigilance demanded by frying, and the timing that made rice sing. The kitchen did not coddle mistakes; it corrected them. Learning there was iterative: taste, adjust, test again.

At the same time, social constraints shaped possibilities. Jim Crow's architecture of segregation set firm limits on formal education and public access, but culinary work occupied a complicated space. Service labor, often relegated to Black women, offered limited social recognition yet provided a route to economic independence. Lena recognized both the constraint and the opportunity. Instead of accepting domestic work as a ceiling, she began to imagine it as groundwork for enterprise. If others presented cooking as a private skill, she started to see it as a transferable, teachable, and ultimately marketable craft.

Even as tradition taught her labor, curiosity pushed Lena beyond inherited recipes. She watched commercial kitchens in the city—hotel dining rooms, bespoke caterers, and the gleaming backs of restaurants—and noted differences in scale and technique. How did professionals keep consistency across hundreds of plates? What administrative strategies kept a lunch service from spiraling into chaos? The answers to those questions fascinated her. She kept notebooks—simple lists at first, then measurements and timings—and began treating culinary practice as a set of procedures that could be studied and improved.

Religion and community institutions further shaped her early sensibilities. Church suppers and charity dinners demanded both flavor and economy; cooks were judged not just on taste but on their ability to feed crowds. Those events trained Lena in menu planning, portion control, and the logistics of large-scale feeding. When a kitchen must feed an entire parish, improvisation must coexist with reliability. That combination taught her how to balance creativity with the managerial demands that running a professional kitchen would later require.

Music and social life intersected with food in ways that deepened Lena's cultural literacy. Jazz, blues, and Creole melodies accompanied many meals, and she learned that rhythm and timing in a kitchen resembled musical phrasing: a pause for a simmer, a quick flourish to finish a sauce. This sensibility made food performance as much about tempo as about taste. Guests didn't just eat; they experienced orchestrated moments—entrées that arrived at the exact point when conversation hummed, desserts that closed a meal like a satisfying cadential chord. Lena absorbed that performative element and made it part of her professional imagination.

Early work experience added practical discipline. Whether assisting in neighborhood eateries or taking on small catering gigs, she learned the demands of customer expectations and the economics of turning food into a business. Portion costing, supplier relationships, and the management of spoilage entered her repertoire. These early responsibilities taught a crucial lesson: culinary excellence must be partnered with sound business practice if it is to sustain livelihoods and scale effect. In Lena's early years, the seed of entrepreneurship took root as she watched how successful kitchens combined artistry with fiscal sense.

Education in formal institutions lay beyond the immediate neighborhood, yet Lena's ambitions reached toward it. She began to see technical training as an escalation of what she already knew—an opportunity to transform tacit knowledge into accredited skill. The decision to pursue formal culinary study later in life was seeded in these earliest exposures: she wanted techniques standardized, recipes tested under controlled conditions, and authority that could travel beyond the kitchen's doorstep. That impulse to professionalize—turning oral knowledge into documented practice—would become one of her signature moves.

Throughout these formative years, Lena cultivated a particular blend of respect for tradition and openness to innovation. She honored family recipes and community methods while remaining alert to new tools, storage methods, and marketing possibilities. That balanced stance allowed her to navigate the cultural politics of Creole cuisine—respecting its origins while showing that it could thrive in modern markets and media. Her early life in New Orleans taught her the technical foundations of flavor and the social strategies of influence: a heady combination that prepared her to transform local mastery into public authority.

# Chapter two

# Learning the Craft: From Local Kitchens to Culinary School

Learning the craft for Lena Richard was a deliberate climb from the lived knowledge of neighborhood kitchens to the disciplined technique of a formal culinary education. Her apprenticeship began in the bustle of home cooking and small food businesses—places where instinct ruled but where survival required dependable results. Those early jobs taught the work ethic of feeding people on schedule, the economy of stretching ingredients without sacrificing flavor, and the quiet pride of a dish well executed. But Lena sought more than competence; she wanted mastery that could be taught, measured, and replicated. That ambition sent her beyond familiar hearths and into classrooms designed to convert craft into certified skill.

In neighborhood kitchens, Lena learned at the elbow of cooks who had theirs passed down through touch and memory. Techniques there were rarely written; timing and feel guided every move. A roux was judged by color and scent rather than by minutes on a clock; a sauce's thickness was measured by how it fell from a spoon, not by grams. These tactile assessments produced excellent food, but they did not always translate easily to large-scale service or to students who needed explicit steps. Lena absorbed the tacit knowledge—how oil heats differently depending on pot metal, how rice can be coaxed into proper texture by precise water ratios—and she also began to record those practices. Notebooks replaced mental notes; measurements replaced hunches. Turning whispering know-how into written method was the first step toward professionalization.

Work in commercial kitchens taught another layer: organization. A home cook improvises around a single meal; a restaurant must produce dozens of consistent plates within minutes. Lena watched how brigade systems divided labor, how mise en place kept chaos at bay, and how timing synchronized cooks like players in a chamber ensemble. She learned inventory control—not as a distant accounting exercise but as a practical tool to prevent spoilage and manage costs. Suppliers, delivery schedules, and seasonal availability shaped daily prep lists. These logistical skills broadened her understanding of what culinary success demanded: not just delicious food, but predictable supply chains and efficient workflows.

Exposure to formal hospitality settings—hotels, upscale restaurants, private catering—revealed standards she admired and wanted to adopt. Uniformity of portion, exacting temperature control, and plated presentation in these venues contrasted with the improvisational charm of neighborhood fare. Lena studied these differences with the eye of both craftsman and entrepreneur. She asked practical questions: How did chefs produce identical sauces at scale? What food-safety measures ensured customer health? Which accounting practices allowed a kitchen to be profitable? Each answer suggested a gap between raw skill and professional practice she was determined to close.

The decision to attend culinary school was a pivotal moment. At institutions like the Fannie Farmer School of Cookery—an establishment that prized measurement, sanitation, and textbook methods—Lena found the vocabulary she needed. Where heritage kitchens passed know-how by example, Fannie Farmer insisted on ratios, temperatures, and step-by-step procedures. That language reframed cooking from folklore into science. Recipes became experiments with controlled variables; success meant repeatable results irrespective of who executed the dish. For Lena, formal training did not erase cultural tradition; it translated it into a format that could be taught to others and defended against misinterpretation.

In school, she learned the mechanics behind flavor. The Maillard reaction ceased to be a mysterious browning and became a predictable chemical interaction to be coaxed by heat and time. Stocks were no longer vague reductions but measured infusions governed by simmer times and specific water-to-bone ratios. Baking—where precision matters most—trained her to weigh flour, to set temperatures accurately, and to understand leavening agents in mathematical terms. These skills were practical: a consistent gumbo base, a reproducible béchamel, breads that rose evenly. More importantly, they provided credibility. Credentials mattered in a marketplace that valued standardized training when hiring cooks for professional kitchens.

Sanitation and food safety emerged as unexpected but indispensable pillars of professionalism. Classroom instruction emphasized storage temperatures, cross-contamination prevention, and cleanliness protocols—areas that could mean the difference between a profitable business and costly closures. Lena absorbed these lessons with pragmatic seriousness. For someone building a public-facing enterprise, the ability to present food that was as safe as it was flavorful built trust with clients and regulators. Those procedural standards also supported her later work teaching students how to run their own kitchens with confidence.

The methodology of culinary science also reshaped Lena's approach to recipes. Instead of a list of "a pinch" here and "a handful" there, she began to compile precise ingredient lists and timing cues. This shift made it possible to reproduce classic Creole dishes with fidelity across cooks and venues. Translating oral tradition into measured formulas preserved cultural specificity while making it accessible to novices and to commercial production. That process of codification was a quiet revolution: it legalized Creole technique as teachable know-how rather than mere inherited taste.

Beyond technique, culinary school offered professional rituals and exposure to wider networks. Students learned to maintain journals of trials and adjustments, to present dishes for critique, and to accept iterative failure as part of improvement. Peer critiques honed presentation skills; instructors introduced business concepts that linked the kitchen to markets. The social capital gained—contacts with suppliers, references from instructors, and familiarity with trade conventions—equipped Lena with tools beyond the stove. She began to think in systems, imagining not just a single restaurant but the possibility of multiple revenue streams: teaching, catering, publishing.

The social dynamics of being a Black woman seeking formal training in a segregated era added friction and sharpened resolve. Access to certain institutions was constrained; acceptance into culinary programs could require negotiations, travel, or financial sacrifice. Lena's decision to pursue professional education was therefore a strategic investment: time and money spent learning technical language that would later translate into authority and business opportunities. That authority mattered in a marketplace where journeymen and managers often dismissed cooks trained only by family practice. A certificate signaled seriousness and opened doors to commercial contracts that would otherwise remain closed.

Returning to New Orleans with formal credentials, Lena faced the practical challenge of applying textbook methods to the variable realities of Southern ingredients and equipment. Local humidity affects dough; seasonal produce demands menu adjustments; supplier inconsistencies require on-the-fly adaptations. Her training had taught her how to anticipate and adjust for these variables: which formulas could be scaled, what tolerances to allow, and how to document substitution strategies. Using scientific method in the kitchen, she created process manuals, prep lists, and standardized recipes that made it possible for others to reproduce her results reliably.

Teaching became a natural extension of her training. The skills she acquired made Lena an excellent instructor: she could demonstrate a technique, explain the scientific rationale, and provide measured recipes students could follow. Her classes emphasized reproducibility and professional standards—students learned not just to cook a dish but to run a kitchen. That pedagogy multiplied her impact: every student who adopted her methods carried them into new kitchens, amplifying the professional practices she championed.

The leap from local kitchens to culinary school thus represented both technical refinement and strategic agency.

Lena translated community inheritance into institutional knowledge, blending respect for heritage with the rigor of measurement and systems thinking. Those years of study and practice equipped her to professionalize Creole cuisine, to teach it to others, and to scale it into a business model that could survive in a segregated economy. Her education did not hollow out tradition; it strengthened it—making recipes teachable, techniques auditable, and craft transferable.

# Chapter three

# The Fannie Farmer Experience: Mastering the Art of Cooking

Enrolling at the Fannie Farmer School of Cookery marked a turning point in Lena Richard's life—a deliberate shift from instinct-driven practice to disciplined, repeatable technique. The school's emphasis on measurement, sanitation, and method offered her a vocabulary that transformed kitchen lore into teachable craft. For someone raised in the improvisational world of Creole home cooking, this education furnished a toolkit that made culinary artistry portable: reproducible recipes, standardized procedures, and professional habits that could be passed on to students or scaled for a business.

Fannie Farmer's curriculum insisted that cooks understand *why* a process worked, not merely *that* it did. That epistemology appealed to Richard's practical mind. In class she learned to quantify texture and timing—how many minutes a stock should simmer to yield a clear, flavorful base; the precise ratio of fat to flour for a dependable roux; the temperatures that coax yeast into predictable rises. Those particulars would later let her translate a grandmother's touch into an instruction set anyone could follow. The pedagogical shift was subtle but profound: cooking ceased to be exclusive intuition and became a kind of applied science.

Technique was only one side of the education. The school reinforced habits of professional conduct that are invisible on a dinner plate but decisive in business. Punctuality, cleanliness, record-keeping, and respect for flow all mattered. Students were taught to mise en place not as a ritual but as a productivity system: chopping, measuring, and arranging ingredients ahead of time to reduce error during service. Richard adopted these routines and, more importantly, learned to teach them. In her later cooking school, these operational disciplines underpinned students' ability to handle large events, manage staff, and maintain consistent product quality—all essential for earning contracts and building reputation.

A surprising lesson for many who crossed from informal kitchens to formal classrooms was the centrality of sanitation. Fannie Farmer emphasized food safety at a time when such standards were not universally enforced. Temperature control, proper storage, and avoidance of cross-contamination were presented not as bureaucratic annoyances but as moral obligations—ensuring customers' health and protecting an enterprise from ruin. For Richard, who intended to operate in public venues, these protocols were a kind of insurance. Demonstrating adherence to sanitation standards made her more trustworthy to clients and regulators alike.

The baking modules were particularly transformative. Baking demands precision: a slight mismeasure can collapse a cake, alter crumb structure, or ruin leavening. Under supervised practice, Richard learned to weigh ingredients, calibrate ovens, and interpret clues—such as the color of a crust or the bounce of a loaf—that signal doneness. Those lessons tightened her approach to all kitchen work. Recipes in her later cookbooks and teaching materials reflected exact measurements and clear steps, enabling reproducibility across cooks of varying experience.

Another vital component of her training involved menu planning and cost control. Successful kitchens balance culinary ambition with financial reality. Fannie Farmer's instruction in portion sizing, yield calculation, and supplier selection equipped Richard to estimate cost per plate, to design menus that matched budget constraints, and to minimize waste. That savvy allowed her to price services competitively while maintaining profitability—an essential skill for a restaurateur or caterer operating in a segregated economy with delicate margins.

Demonstration skills formed part of the pedagogy as well. Students learned to present dishes with confidence, to explain techniques to curious onlookers, and to field questions without faltering. This modality anticipated Richard's later career as a public culinary teacher and broadcaster. The ability to communicate culinary concepts plainly—translating chemical interactions or timing cues into conversational language—made her an effective instructor and a credible voice in media. Her television audiences later benefited not only from recipes but from that clear, composed delivery honed in classroom drills.

Critical thinking about ingredients and substitutions was another classroom advantage. The school taught students to analyze the function of each component: fats for tenderness, acids for brightness, starches for thickening. Understanding these roles allowed Richard to adapt recipes intelligently when faced with local variations in produce or equipment. In the American South, humidity, seasonal supply, and the sometimes unpredictable quality of shipments required flexibility. Training in food chemistry let her create tolerances—ranges of acceptable variation—rather than brittle instructions, ensuring consistent outcomes even when conditions deviated from textbook ideals.

Exposure to professional tools and commercial-grade equipment demystified settings and scale. Where neighborhood kitchens often relied on whatever pots and ranges were available, the school provided experience with standardized ovens, steam equipment, and portioning devices. Learning how these machines performed under different loads accelerated her capacity to design menus and prep schedules for larger services. She learned how to convert a home recipe into a banquet formula: multiplying ingredient lists, adjusting cooking times for larger volumes, and sequencing production to maintain freshness across service windows.

Pedagogical critique sessions sharpened her judgment. Presenting a dish for instructor review taught her to accept constructive criticism and to iterate. Instructors pointed out imbalances—too much salt, underdeveloped reduction, or uneven texture—and students were expected to refine their methods. That iterative loop instilled a tolerance for controlled failure: an experimental mindset that tests variations, documents results, and converges on better technique. This systematic refinement translated directly into her classroom approach later; she taught students to treat mistakes as data, not as defeat.

The Fannie Farmer environment also introduced Lena to culinary networks and credentialing that mattered in the marketplace. A certificate from an established institution signaled competence to hotels, caterers, and prospective patrons who might otherwise discount a cook's skill based on background. For a Black woman operating in the segregated South, such credentials provided leverage. They did not erase racism, but they furnished tools for asserting professional legitimacy in markets where prejudice might otherwise deflect opportunity.

The cultural translation was equally important. Instructors encouraged students to study classic French techniques—mother sauces, stocks, sauces reduction—which formed a technical backbone for many professional kitchens. Lena saw these techniques not as threats to Creole identity but as instruments she could fold into local tradition, enriching gumbo and étouffée with greater textural control and refined presentation. She blended Fannie Farmer's systematic methods with Creole flavor principles, creating a hybrid competence: dishes that honored regional roots while meeting professional standards for consistency and elegance.

Finally, the school instilled an ethic of teaching. Fannie Farmer's pedagogical model was not merely about personal advancement; it was a lineage meant to be passed on. Students were trained to document, to explain, and to structure lessons for novices. Lena internalized that orientation. When she later opened her own cooking school, the emphasis on measured instruction, student practice, and vocational preparation echoed the methods she had absorbed. Her students benefited from an educational model that turned oral inheritance into credentialed skill, empowering them to pursue careers with confidence and technique.

The Fannie Farmer experience, therefore, was less a rejection of Lena's heritage than an elevation of it. It supplied a grammar for documenting and teaching Creole practice, tools for operating at commercial scale, and the managerial insight needed to make kitchens profitable and reliable. In those classrooms she sharpened taste into technique and transmuted family knowledge into professional authority—capabilities that would sustain her entrepreneurial ventures and help transform how Creole cuisine was taught, sold, and respected.

# Chapter four

# Coming Home with New Skills and Bigger Dreams

Returning to New Orleans after formal culinary training felt less like coming home and more like bringing a toolbox into a workshop that already hummed with possibility. Lena Richard arrived with measured recipes, sanitation protocols, and a professional cadence that contrasted with the improvisational rhythms of neighborhood kitchens. That contrast was not a rejection of tradition; it was an expansion of it. She layered textbook precision over inherited technique, and in doing so she opened doors not only for herself but for the many cooks who would follow her path.

The first practical change was how she organized her workspace. Where kitchens once relied on memory and instinct, Lena introduced routines that made results repeatable. She instituted mise en place as a discipline rather than a suggestion: ingredients measured, equipment staged, timelines plotted. This practice turned chaotic services into predictable operations. It also freed creative energy—when the basics were handled reliably, cooks could focus on flavor innovation rather than firefighting. Her teams learned to value preparation as much as the final plate.

Documentation became an instrument of empowerment. Lena kept recipe cards that listed exact measurements and step-by-step directions, not vague notes scribbled in margins. Those cards served two functions: they preserved family recipes in a standardized form, and they provided teachable templates for students who lacked years of informal apprenticeship. By committing techniques to paper, she made culinary knowledge portable. Anyone with access to her notes could recreate a dish with fidelity, which broadened the audience for Creole cuisine beyond tight family circles.

Her return also sharpened an entrepreneurial imagination. Seeing a market that appreciated well-executed regional dishes, she began to think beyond one-off meals and toward enterprises: a cooking school, a catering business, and eventually a line of packaged foods. Each idea required systems—procurement channels, pricing frameworks, labor plans—that her classroom training helped her design. She approached these ventures like a problem set: identify constraints, propose interventions, model outcomes, and iterate. That methodical approach distinguished her from contemporaries who relied solely on culinary flair.

Community response encouraged risk-taking. Patrons who remembered her family's cooking noticed a new reliability: the same gumbo on different nights, the identical sauce at afternoon affairs. Word-of-mouth spread not only because the food tasted excellent but because customers learned they could depend on consistent quality. That trust translated into contracts—catered luncheons, society events, and church suppers—that provided steady revenue. Lena reinvested those returns into equipment and training, building capacity to serve larger events with the same attention to detail.

Her cooking school came from a belief that craft should be teachable and that economic opportunity should be intentional. She structured classes to bridge kitchen technique and business know-how: students practiced standardized recipes, documented yields, and learned how to price menus. Financial literacy became part of the curriculum—how to calculate cost per serving, manage inventory turnover, and forecast seasonal purchases. Those lessons made graduates attractive hires for restaurants and enabled some to start small businesses of their own. In this way, Lena's classroom functioned as workforce development disguised as cooking instruction.

At the same time, she remained connected to local suppliers. She cultivated relationships with farmers, grocers, and fishmongers, learning their cycles and preferences. These ties ensured steady access to key ingredients and allowed her to negotiate prices beneficial for both parties. Her procurement strategies were practical: buy seasonally to control cost, form partnerships that guaranteed quality, and maintain slender margins balanced by volume and efficiency. Such practices made her operations resilient to supply disruptions and responsive to community needs.

Marketing was another area where she applied new skills. Lena learned how to present menus in clear, appealing language and how to format recipes for print. Her cookbook, for instance, transformed classroom staples into a published resource that extended her brand. She designed covers with practical appeal and wrote instructions intended for the general reader, not just professional cooks. The book functioned as both instruction and advertisement: it taught readers how to reproduce Creole flavors and sent potential students and customers her way. That dual purpose made publishing a strategic career move rather than a vanity project.

She also navigated social boundaries with a savvy blend of diplomacy and firmness. In segregated settings, the act of serving integrated clientele or training Black students for commercial employment required careful negotiation. Lena cultivated allies among sympathetic patrons, while also asserting clear standards in her classrooms and kitchens. She used professionalism to shift conversations: when food arrived on time and met exacting expectations, arguments based on prejudice often lost traction. That tactic—raise the level of work until bias was practically inconvenient—became a subtle form of social leverage.

Scale required managerial innovations. Lena learned to delegate, to create positions with clear responsibilities, and to design workflows that allowed multiple dishes to be produced simultaneously without sacrificing quality. She trained supervisors to replicate her standards and to perform quality checks. Those roles made her business less dependent on any single person's skill and more reliant on institutional procedures. By building capacity, she increased the reach of her culinary voice while also creating jobs and career pathways in a constrained labor market.

Experimentation continued to be a part of her practice. Standardization did not mean stagnation. She tested ingredient substitutions, adjusted spicing for different palates, and refined techniques for durability in packaged products. When developing frozen meals, for example, she wrestled with texture maintenance and flavor retention—problems that demanded both culinary knowledge and practical ingenuity. She prototyped recipes, recorded outcomes, and iterated until results met both taste and shelf-stability requirements. That process blended the laboratory mindset of measured experiments with the sensibility of a seasoned cook.

Teaching remained central to her identity. The classroom became an engine of social mobility: students learned not only how to cook but how to manage time, keep records, and treat customers with respect. Lena emphasized soft skills—communication, punctuality, and presentation—that employers valued but which were often absent in informal training. She also instilled a discipline of continuous improvement: taste, adjust, and document. Her pedagogy aimed to create professionals who could enter diverse culinary roles and hold them with dignity.

Her public visibility grew. Local radio and community events offered platforms to showcase her recipes and to promote her classes. These appearances amplified demand and diversified income streams. She understood media as an amplifier: a short radio segment or a well-placed newspaper mention could fill classes and bookings. Lena crafted messages that spoke to practical benefits—time-saving tips, reliable menus, and methods to stretch ingredients—making her advice useful for both home cooks and professionals.

Finally, her return home was marked by a sense of mission. She did not only seek personal success; she wanted to transform perceptions of Creole cuisine and to create opportunities for cooks who had talent but lacked access. Each class she taught, each contract she fulfilled, and each cookbook sold served that purpose. In a world where cultural contributions were easily overlooked, Lena built institutions—kitchens, schools, and businesses—that made the value of her community's culinary expertise visible, transferable, and economically viable.

# Chapter five

# Breaking Barriers in the Restaurant World

Breaking into the restaurant business as a Black woman in early twentieth-century New Orleans was not simply a matter of opening a door; it was an exercise in navigation, persuasion, and sustained excellence. Lena Richard's approach combined culinary mastery with shrewd business sense, strategic relationship-building, and an unflinching focus on standards. She didn't merely fit into existing structures—she bent them, carving out spaces where talent and reliability counted more than the prejudices that otherwise shaped who could serve, who could dine, and who could profit from food culture.

The first obstacle was access: professional kitchens, upscale dining rooms, and commercial suppliers often operated like closed circuits. Contracts for catering, permits for certain neighborhoods, or lines of credit from banks were frequently denied or conditioned by race and gender. Lena met these barriers by converting craft into proof. Her menus, precise recipes, and consistent product quality became demonstrable evidence of competency. Where access was blocked by assumptions, her work presented an alternative argument: the food reliably arrived on time, tasted as promised, and satisfied paying customers. Over time that record made it harder for gatekeepers to dismiss her requests for space, ingredients, or contracts.

Location mattered too. New Orleans' dining scene offered different contours — from modest neighborhood joints to grand hotel dining rooms frequented by affluent patrons. Lena chose venues that maximized visibility and credibility. Running establishments in neighborhoods that connected to both local communities and visiting elites allowed her to serve diverse clientèle and to show that Creole cuisine could satisfy high standards. That strategic placement created a bridge: patrons who tasted her food in one setting would ask for it in others, and word-of-mouth began to move across social lines.

Hiring and training staff was another terrain where Lena made deliberate choices that advanced both quality and opportunity. She recruited from local talent pools and invested in instruction that emphasized consistency. Her employees learned to execute dishes to exacting specifications, to follow sanitation protocols, and to manage service flow. This emphasis on reproducibility meant that the business was not dependent on a single cook's idiosyncrasies. It also provided pathways for Black cooks to gain professional experience and, in some cases, to move into supervisory roles.

By professionalizing kitchen work, she elevated the position of service labor into a respectable career trajectory.

Dealing with suppliers and vendors required negotiation skills seldom taught in culinary school. Lena cultivated relationships with fishmongers, farmers, and grocers, learning their rhythms and creating reciprocal arrangements. Those relationships helped stabilize costs and ensured the quality of perishable ingredients that define Creole dishes. When suppliers trusted her payment practices and volume projections, they treated her as a reliable account rather than a marginal client. That status translated into better selection, more favorable credit terms, and timely deliveries—practical advantages that reinforced the food's consistency.

Marketing and reputation management played a crucial role. Lena mastered the art of presentation and the power of narrative. Menus were not just lists; they were careful statements about taste, technique, and provenance. She used print—cookbooks, flyers, newspaper mentions—to extend her brand beyond the dining room. Public demonstrations and speaking engagements reinforced her authority and brought new customers through the door. Media exposure, modest by today's standards but influential then, helped normalize the idea of a Black woman running a reputable food business and reaching customers beyond her immediate community.

Regulatory friction was a persistent threat. Licenses, health inspections, and zoning laws operated in a system that could be applied unequally. Lena addressed this by embracing compliance as a competitive edge. Sanitation, record-keeping, and transparent accounting became not merely obligations but selling points. Her kitchens displayed cleanliness alongside culinary creativity, and that visible professionalism won favor with inspectors and patrons alike. In a climate where prejudice could be cloaked as bureaucratic concern, adherence to standards offered a defensible position that protected business continuity.

Social dynamics at the table often mirrored societal fault lines. Some patrons expected a certain deference from a Black server or cook; others were curious or approving. Lena navigated these dynamics by insisting on dignity and by setting the tone in her establishments. Service staff were trained to be courteous without self-effacement; chefs communicated expertise without apologizing for origin. Creating an environment that combined warmth with competence helped shift patron expectations. Over time, repeat customers came to value the food and the experience more than any preconceived notions about who prepared it.

Scaling operations required both managerial sophistication and an appetite for risk. Lena tested expansion through catering large events and experimenting with prepared-food production. Scaling meant confronting problems of logistics:

how to transport temperature-sensitive dishes, how to coordinate staff for simultaneous services, and how to price offerings to cover overhead while remaining affordable. Her solutions—detailed prep schedules, staging plans, and contingency protocols—read like a playbook for small-business resilience. Each successful large-scale engagement proved the business model and attracted more ambitious contracts.

Financial prudence underpinned every advancement. Lena balanced reinvestment in equipment and training with the need to maintain cash flow. She negotiated credit, kept close tabs on cost per plate, and designed menus that accounted for seasonal pricing. This financial discipline allowed her to weather slow periods and to invest in quality where it mattered most—better ingredients, improved cookware, and staff development. In an environment where economic marginalization could quickly sink an enterprise, her fiscal habits created a buffer against volatility.

Perhaps most impactful was the example she set. By operating with excellence, hiring and training community members, and promoting the craft of Creole cooking, Lena redefined what success could look like for Black restaurateurs. She demonstrated that culinary heritage could be a foundation for entrepreneurship rather than a relegation to menial service. Her restaurants and ventures became models that others could emulate—proof that, with technique, preparation, and organizational clarity, barriers could be narrowed. In doing so, she shifted cultural perceptions about who belonged in the kitchen and who could profit from it.

Her presence in spaces where food and power intersected quietly altered norms. Hosts who once expected anonymous labor began to reckon with skill as a form of capital. Local institutions—churches, clubs, and civic groups—started hiring her for events that signaled prestige, and those choices carried social meaning. For aspiring cooks and restaurateurs, Lena's example broadcast a message: identity need not be destiny; with determination and sound practice, food could be a vehicle for economic and social mobility.

Throughout these efforts, she managed a delicate choreography—honoring tradition while meeting modern expectations, creating jobs while maintaining profitability, and seeking visibility without courting unnecessary confrontation. That balance required continuous adaptation and a refusal to accept excuses. Each plate that left her kitchen affirmed not just taste but strategy: culinary excellence married to business acumen. The restaurant world's barriers were stubborn, but Lena's response was methodical: build quality that cannot be ignored, teach standards that can be replicated, and run an enterprise so reliable it compels recognition.

# Chapter six

# The Cookbook That Made History

When Lena Richard set out to write a cookbook, she was doing more than collecting recipes—she was making a case that Creole cooking deserved the same measured, professional treatment as any classical cuisine. The project began in practical, determined fashion: Richard dictated more than three hundred recipes, menus, and kitchen tips to her daughter, Marie, who transcribed them for a typist. That labor—oral memory translated into written instruction—was itself an act of preservation and power, turning household knowledge into a resource anyone could follow.

She first self-published her collection in 1939 as *Lena Richard's Cook Book*, a compact manual aimed at cooks who wanted dependable results. The book wore its purpose plainly: exact measurements, step-by-step directions, and menus designed for everything from modest family suppers to large social functions. It reflected Richard's dual apprenticeship—the tactile wisdom of New Orleans kitchens and the disciplined technique she refined at the Fannie Farmer School of Cookery—so the text moved between soul and science with deliberate ease. That hybrid voice made the recipes both authentic and reproducible, a combination rare in cookbooks of the era.

Self-publishing required hustle. Richard financed the initial print run herself and then took to the road to sell copies, treating each sale like both income and publicity. On a single monthlong tour she reportedly sold hundreds of volumes door-to-door and at events—an effort that demonstrated entrepreneurial grit as much as culinary authority. Those early sales helped prove there was a market for a cookbook that centered Creole technique written by a Black woman—a claim that soon attracted broader attention.

A key turning point came when influential food editors and advocates amplified the book's reach. With help from supporters in the press, her work landed before Houghton Mifflin, which republished the volume in 1940 under the title *New Orleans Cook Book*. The reissue gave the recipes a national imprint and moved Richard from local celebrity to a figure whose name appeared in prominent publishing catalogs. However, the reissue also reflected the uneasy racial politics of the period: the publisher removed Richard's portrait from the book's interior and attached an introduction by a well-known white Southern writer—moves that granted legitimacy in white publishing circles while partially erasing visible traces of the author's identity. That tension—the leap into mainstream recognition that also required cultural compromise—became part of the book's complex legacy.

The cookbook itself is a study in practical mastery. Recipes ranged from elegant pastries and delicate tea treats to robust stews, seafood classics, and large-event menus—reflecting the full range of New Orleans' culinary life. Richard's directions favored clarity: standardized measurements, recommended equipment, and suggested timing. The text anticipated the needs of both novice home cooks and working professionals, with instructions that could be scaled for a single family meal or for the bustling demands of catering and hotel service. That versatility helped the book function as both a teaching manual and a business tool.

Beyond technical instruction, the book served as a cultural ledger. By committing traditional Creole recipes to print—not as exotic curiosities but as tested procedures—Richard asserted ownership over a cuisine often appropriated or misattributed. Her measured approach validated Creole technique as systematic knowledge, not mere taste memory. For Black cooks and students in her classes, the cookbook became curriculum: a portable syllabus that translated apprenticeship into credentialed practice. In a segregated society where vocational pathways were limited, this codification opened tangible doors.

The timing of publication mattered. The late 1930s and early 1940s were an era of expanding mass media and changing food technologies—freezing, canning, and radio were reshaping how people cooked and thought about meals.

Richard's cookbook arrived at that junction and became a platform for other ventures: her public demonstrations, radio segments, and later television appearances often referenced recipes in the book, creating an integrated brand that moved from print to airwaves. The cookbook was not an isolated artifact; it served as the backbone of a career that included restaurants, a cooking school, and even a frozen-food line. Each new medium amplified the cookbook's reach and reinforced the idea that Creole cuisine belonged in national culinary conversations.

Critically, the book's structure reflected Richard's pedagogical commitments. Where many recipe collections left technique implied, she spelled out methods in ways students could adopt—how to build a stock, how to judge a roux by color and smell, and how to plan menus that balanced cost and flavor. Her emphasis on sanitation and consistency echoed her training and professional priorities; she treated kitchen practice as a form of vocational expertise rather than mere household advice. For graduates of her cooking school, the cookbook served as a bridge between classroom drills and the demands of commercial kitchens.

The book also sparked broader conversations about authorship and representation. When a major publisher repackaged the text for a national audience, debates emerged—subtle then, louder now—about how Black culinary contributions were framed for mainstream consumption. The removal of Richard's photographic image from the Houghton Mifflin edition, and the placing of a white writer's introduction, illustrated how editorial choices could both elevate and erase. Contemporary scholars and food historians have since reexamined those editorial moves, noting how they reflect broader patterns in American publishing and cultural gatekeeping. Recovering Richard's original voice—her own title page, her named dedication, and her direct instructions—has become part of the modern project of restoring credit where it was obscured.

Commercially, the cookbook's reputation endured. Copies of the 1940 edition became sought-after items, and the text has been reprinted and anthologized for modern audiences interested in Creole authenticity and culinary history. More importantly, the methods it preserved shaped professional practice: chefs who traced lineage in New Orleans kitchens cite the book as a touchstone for technique and menu planning. Historians now point to the cookbook as an early example of Black culinary entrepreneurship in the twentieth century—an instance of cultural labor translated into marketable knowledge.

The tactile story of how the cookbook was made matters as much as its content. The act of dictation—Lena speaking recipes from memory while her daughter wrote them down—captures an intergenerational collaboration that is itself emblematic of how culinary tradition moves forward.

That handwritten-to-printed trajectory preserved family and community know-how in a form that outlived a single kitchen and allowed Creole technique to enter classrooms, restaurant test kitchens, and American households. The book's pages became a conduit: a way for a regional cuisine shaped by multiple diasporas to be taught, tasted, and taken seriously within the modern culinary economy.

In short, *Lena Richard's* cookbook did more than collect dishes; it rewired expectations about who could teach, publish, and professionalize American regional food. The volume's blend of technical clarity, cultural stewardship, and entrepreneurial orientation helped transform private practice into public influence—setting a template for later Black women chefs who would make media appearances, publish cookbooks, and run successful culinary enterprises.

# Chapter seven

# Cooking for the Airwaves: Radio and Television Stardom

Lena Richard's transition from kitchen to microphone was more than a career pivot; it was a transformation of influence. She understood early on that food could be more than sustenance—it could be storytelling, culture, and connection. The moment she stepped into the world of radio, she recognized an opportunity not only to teach recipes but to assert the professional legitimacy of Creole cuisine and, more importantly, of herself as a Black woman in a medium dominated by white voices. Her radio debut was not flashy—it was deliberate, disciplined, and carefully planned, much like her approach to the kitchen. Every word, every instruction, was designed to inform, empower, and engage listeners.

Radio demanded clarity. Unlike in-person demonstrations, there were no visual cues, no aromas to guide the audience. Lena had to translate tactile knowledge into precise, descriptive language that painted a picture in the listener's mind. She described textures, aromas, and techniques with the same exacting detail she used in her cookbook, but now filtered for auditory learning. She explained the proper way to make a roux, the subtle difference between a light and dark gumbo stock, and the timing of seasoning additions, all while keeping her tone approachable and inviting. Listeners weren't just learning recipes—they were experiencing her craft through her voice, building trust in her expertise.

The challenge was balancing professional technique with accessibility. Lena recognized that her audience included both seasoned cooks and home chefs who might never have set foot in a formal kitchen. She adapted her instruction accordingly, breaking down complex steps into manageable segments while maintaining the integrity of Creole cuisine. She emphasized that precision need not be intimidating, that proper measurement and timing could yield extraordinary results without requiring years of apprenticeship. This approach made her radio show not only educational but empowering, providing practical skills to a wide spectrum of listeners.

Her charisma was subtle but compelling. Lena's demeanor conveyed confidence without arrogance. She radiated calm authority, demonstrating that mastery could coexist with warmth. That blend of professionalism and approachability made listeners feel capable, inspiring them to try new techniques and flavors. She also peppered her broadcasts with cultural anecdotes, connecting recipes to New Orleans traditions, family gatherings, and historical context. In doing so, she created a multidimensional experience: education, entertainment, and cultural preservation all in one broadcast.

Transitioning to television amplified both the stakes and the potential impact. Television introduced a visual component, demanding that Lena not only instruct but also demonstrate with elegance and efficiency. Her sets were meticulously organized: ingredients pre-measured, utensils aligned, surfaces spotless, and timing planned to the second. Every movement was deliberate, reinforcing her credibility while allowing the audience to follow along effortlessly. Her camera presence reflected the same values she instilled in her classrooms—poise, precision, and clarity—making complicated techniques accessible to viewers of varying skill levels.

Television also allowed her to showcase the beauty of Creole cuisine. Colorful sauces, vibrant vegetables, and artful presentation came alive on screen, providing an additional layer of sensory engagement. By pairing visual demonstration with her authoritative narration, Lena elevated the perception of regional cuisine from home-cooked fare to professional culinary artistry. This visibility was particularly powerful in challenging societal expectations of both Black women and Southern cooking. Audiences were invited to appreciate the sophistication, technique, and heritage embedded in each dish, effectively rewriting assumptions about who could define taste and culture in America.

Strategically, Lena leveraged her media appearances to extend her influence beyond the broadcast itself. Each show referenced her cookbook, creating a feedback loop that drove sales and built her brand. Listeners and viewers who were inspired by her demonstrations were motivated to purchase her book, attend her cooking classes, or hire her for events. This synergy between media exposure and entrepreneurship exemplified her foresight: broadcasting was not simply a platform for recognition, but a conduit for sustainable business growth.

Her presence in media also carried social significance. At a time when segregation and systemic racism limited visibility for Black professionals, Lena's voice and image reached households that might never have encountered her otherwise. She subtly challenged norms, demonstrating skill, professionalism, and authority in spaces that were rarely occupied by women of color. Each broadcast was a small act of advocacy, asserting that culinary mastery transcended race, gender, and geography. Audiences, both Black and white, came to respect her expertise because it was undeniable—consistent, polished, and rooted in authentic experience.

The preparation for radio and television was itself a disciplined process. Lena approached each segment as she would a complex recipe: planning ingredients, timing each step, and rehearsing delivery. Mistakes were minimized through meticulous preparation, and she trained assistants to anticipate needs, ensuring smooth broadcasts. This professional rigor reflected her broader ethos: mastery is inseparable from preparation, and success in any public forum requires the same care as success in the kitchen.

Her media work also included interactive elements that engaged the audience. Listeners could send letters with questions, which she answered on air, offering personalized guidance and encouragement. This interaction created a sense of community around her shows, transforming passive consumption into active participation. Fans felt connected to Lena not just as a chef but as a mentor and cultural ambassador. The personal engagement reinforced loyalty, building a network of supporters who became advocates for her cuisine, her classes, and her publications.

Beyond education and visibility, Lena's media presence contributed to the preservation of Creole culinary heritage. Television and radio captured techniques, ingredient combinations, and procedural knowledge that might otherwise have remained local or undocumented. In an era before digital archiving, these broadcasts served as living repositories, transmitting skill and culture across time and space. Young cooks who never visited New Orleans could learn foundational Creole methods, while seasoned chefs gained exposure to regional nuances that might have escaped their training.

The combination of pedagogy, professionalism, and media savvy set Lena Richard apart from her contemporaries. She was not only a practitioner but also a communicator, translator, and strategist. Her broadcasts exemplified the integration of content mastery and audience awareness: she understood what viewers needed, how to deliver it compellingly, and how to leverage exposure into broader opportunities. In doing so, she created a blueprint for future culinary personalities—particularly women and people of color—seeking to combine expertise with public influence.

Lena's work in radio and television thus represented a convergence of artistry, technique, and entrepreneurship. Each broadcast was a performance, a lesson, and a statement of professional identity. By translating the tactile, intimate practice of cooking into an accessible, broadcast-friendly format, she expanded the reach of her culinary philosophy, preserved cultural knowledge, and carved a public space for herself in American culinary history. Her media presence became an extension of her kitchen, a way to educate, inspire, and assert authority across geographic and social boundaries.

Through consistent, thoughtful broadcasting, Lena demonstrated that culinary expertise could be communicated clearly and widely, that Creole cuisine held universal appeal when framed with technique and storytelling, and that a Black woman could command attention and respect in both local and national media. Every listener, every viewer, and every recipe executed at home carried a piece of her influence—turning kitchens across the country into classrooms, and establishing Lena Richard as a pioneering figure whose impact transcended ingredients, pots, and pans.

# Chapter Eight

# Teaching the Next Generation of Chefs

Lena Richard understood that her legacy could extend far beyond the confines of her own kitchen; it was through teaching others that her influence would endure. From early in her career, she recognized that passing knowledge to the next generation was not just about recipes—it was about cultivating professionalism, instilling discipline, and nurturing pride in culinary heritage. Her approach to teaching combined technical mastery, entrepreneurial insight, and cultural affirmation, ensuring that every student left her classroom equipped not just to cook, but to thrive in a competitive industry.

Her cooking school in New Orleans was meticulously designed to reflect real-world kitchen operations. Students didn't merely memorize recipes; they learned systems for organizing ingredients, planning menus, and executing multi-course meals under time constraints. Lena emphasized mise en place—preparing every ingredient before cooking—as a foundational skill. She taught her students to anticipate needs, arrange workstations efficiently, and maintain clean, organized kitchens. These practices were not abstract theory; they mirrored the standards she demanded in her own business, creating a seamless pipeline from classroom to professional kitchen.

Instruction under Lena Richard was intensely hands-on. Students followed her through each step, repeating techniques until muscle memory took over. From the precise whisking of sauces to the subtle layering of spices in Creole dishes, Lena ensured that every skill was internalized. Mistakes were treated as learning opportunities rather than failures. She would demonstrate a technique, allow students to replicate it, and then provide constructive feedback—correcting gently but firmly. Her classroom became a laboratory for skill development, where experimentation and adherence to high standards existed in balance.

Beyond technical proficiency, Lena's pedagogy emphasized the importance of consistency and reproducibility. She taught students that a well-executed dish could be replicated in different settings, whether for a family gathering, a restaurant, or a catering order. She drilled the concept that flavor was only part of the equation; timing, temperature, presentation, and sanitation were equally critical. By codifying these elements into repeatable processes, she prepared her students to succeed in professional kitchens, where reputation often depended on delivering reliable results night after night.

Cultural heritage was at the heart of her teaching. Lena encouraged students to understand the historical and regional significance of the dishes they prepared. She shared stories of New Orleans' Creole community, the evolution of recipes passed down through generations, and the influence of African, French, and Spanish traditions. By framing cooking as both craft and cultural preservation, she instilled pride in her students, emphasizing that mastering technique also meant honoring heritage. Every gumbo, étouffée, or praline became a lesson in history as well as flavor.

Lena's training extended beyond the kitchen to professional skills often overlooked in culinary instruction. Students learned how to manage time effectively, communicate clearly with colleagues and clients, and maintain composure under pressure. She taught them to plan menus strategically, calculate food costs, and manage inventory—practical lessons that bridged the gap between cook and entrepreneur. In doing so, she prepared students not just to fill positions, but to lead kitchens, manage catering operations, or even start their own food businesses.

Mentorship was another cornerstone of her educational philosophy. Lena viewed her role not merely as instructor but as guide and advocate. She encouraged students to dream ambitiously, to recognize opportunities, and to persevere in the face of obstacles. Many of her students were women or African American cooks who faced systemic barriers in employment; Lena provided both the skills and the confidence to navigate these challenges. By modeling professionalism and resilience, she created an environment where ambition was nurtured and potential realized.

The school also emphasized creativity within structure. While students mastered fundamental techniques, Lena encouraged them to experiment with flavors, adjust seasonings, and innovate within the framework of Creole cuisine. She taught that true mastery required both adherence to tradition and the courage to adapt. By fostering an environment where innovation was paired with discipline, she helped students develop distinctive culinary voices, preparing them for a marketplace that valued both skill and originality.

Assessment and evaluation were carefully designed to reinforce accountability. Students were regularly tested on technique, menu planning, and execution. Lena graded performance not only on taste but also on organization, cleanliness, timing, and presentation. Feedback was direct yet supportive, aimed at building competence and confidence. Through structured evaluation, students learned to internalize professional standards and to recognize the critical elements that distinguish an amateur cook from a skilled chef.

Community engagement was another integral part of her teaching. Lena often connected classroom instruction with real-world experience, organizing events where students catered for local organizations, family functions, or charity gatherings. These opportunities allowed students to apply their skills under pressure, interact with paying clients, and receive immediate feedback. Beyond skill development, these experiences reinforced lessons in professionalism, client relations, and operational efficiency, providing a holistic education that extended far beyond the textbooks.

Lena also placed significant emphasis on documentation and record-keeping. She encouraged students to maintain detailed notes on recipes, techniques, ingredient sourcing, and preparation methods. This practice trained them to approach cooking as a disciplined, repeatable process rather than a purely intuitive art. By combining memory, measurement, and meticulous record-keeping, she cultivated a generation of chefs who could deliver excellence consistently, replicate signature dishes, and adapt recipes for diverse settings.

Her teaching philosophy emphasized the long-term trajectory of culinary careers. Lena framed each lesson within the broader context of professional growth, business development, and cultural impact. She taught that being a successful chef required more than skill with ingredients; it demanded vision, strategic thinking, and a commitment to excellence. Through instruction, mentorship, and real-world application, she prepared students to become leaders, innovators, and ambassadors of Creole cuisine.

In nurturing the next generation, Lena Richard created a ripple effect that extended far beyond her immediate classroom. Her students carried her techniques, standards, and values into kitchens across New Orleans and beyond. They replicated her methods, opened their own establishments, and in many cases became mentors themselves. Through teaching, Lena ensured that the artistry and professionalism of Creole cooking would not only survive but thrive, influencing countless kitchens, menus, and culinary careers.

Her classrooms were incubators of empowerment. Students were taught to respect themselves, their craft, and the communities they represented. They were prepared to enter professional kitchens with confidence, competence, and cultural awareness. Lena's instruction combined rigorous technical training, entrepreneurial insight, and mentorship, creating a comprehensive learning experience that set a benchmark for culinary education.

Ultimately, teaching was Lena Richard's way of multiplying impact. Every student who learned from her became a carrier of her philosophy, perpetuating her dedication to skill, discipline, and heritage. Through her educational efforts, she created a living legacy—a network of chefs equipped to carry Creole cuisine forward while navigating the challenges of professional kitchens, entrepreneurship, and cultural preservation. Her influence extended well beyond her own achievements, living on in every hand she guided, every kitchen she shaped, and every student she inspired.

# Chapter nine

# Entrepreneurship on a Plate: From Catering to Frozen Foods

Lena Richard's journey into entrepreneurship was fueled by a vision that extended far beyond the stove. She saw the potential of Creole cuisine not just as a cultural artifact but as a marketable product, capable of reaching audiences beyond the walls of her kitchen or her cooking school. Her business ventures—from catering services to frozen food production—demonstrate a rare combination of culinary mastery, strategic planning, and innovative thinking. Each step of her entrepreneurial path reflects an acute understanding of both the opportunities and the constraints she faced as a Black woman in early-to-mid twentieth-century America.

Catering was the first natural extension of her culinary skill. Lena recognized that while restaurants offered steady income, they were bound by location and the limitations of seating capacity. Catering allowed her to reach a broader clientele, including social clubs, civic organizations, and private events. It also provided a testing ground for larger-scale food preparation, demanding precision, timing, and organization on a scale beyond individual orders. From menu conception to execution, she applied the same standards she taught in her classrooms: exact measurements, ingredient quality, and attention to detail. Each successful event reinforced her reputation for excellence and reliability.

Her catering business also required mastering logistics—an often overlooked component of culinary entrepreneurship. Delivering meals to multiple locations, sometimes simultaneously, meant careful planning. Lena developed systems for portioning, packaging, and transporting food so that dishes arrived in optimal condition. Staff training was critical: employees had to understand the subtleties of timing, food handling, and client interaction. Lena approached these operational challenges with the same rigor she applied to cooking, transforming logistical competence into a competitive advantage.

Word-of-mouth and reputation played a pivotal role in scaling her catering enterprise. Lena's meticulous execution ensured that clients returned repeatedly and referred her services to others. Each event became an advertisement for her skill and professionalism. She understood that every plate served, every client interaction, and every catered function contributed to building a brand. By establishing trust and consistency, she positioned her catering business as a premium service that combined culinary excellence with reliability—a rare offering in her era.

Seeing the limitations of perishable catering and restaurant operations, Lena identified an emerging market: frozen foods. The mid-twentieth century brought technological advances in refrigeration and home freezing, creating opportunities to extend the shelf life of prepared meals. Lena recognized that Creole cuisine, with its rich sauces and complex seasoning, could thrive in this new format if packaged and prepared correctly. She pioneered methods to adapt recipes for freezing without compromising flavor or texture—a task that required experimentation, precise control over cooking temperatures, and creative problem-solving.

Frozen food production also demanded entrepreneurial versatility. Lena navigated issues of supply chain management, storage, and distribution while ensuring quality remained uncompromised. She developed packaging solutions that protected the integrity of her dishes, standardized portion sizes, and maintained nutritional and sensory quality. This enterprise required financial acumen: forecasting demand, pricing products appropriately, and managing overhead costs. Lena's capacity to integrate culinary creativity with operational discipline allowed her to seize a market that few others had considered accessible or profitable.

Marketing was an integral part of her expansion into frozen foods. Lena leveraged her reputation from catering, cooking schools, and media appearances to generate interest. Consumers who trusted her cookbooks and radio demonstrations were more likely to purchase her packaged meals. She understood the power of brand continuity: the same standards, expertise, and personality that made her classrooms and catering events successful were embedded in her frozen products. In this way, the business became a holistic extension of her culinary philosophy, creating consistency across multiple platforms.

Innovation was also central to Lena's approach. She experimented with menu variety, portion sizes, and recipes suitable for freezing, often adjusting traditional Creole methods to meet technological constraints without sacrificing authenticity. By doing so, she transformed regional cuisine into a product that could travel across the country, introducing Creole flavors to households far removed from New Orleans. Her frozen meals became a conduit for cultural transmission, demonstrating that entrepreneurship could preserve and amplify culinary heritage.

Her ventures required balancing tradition with modernity. Lena remained faithful to the flavors and techniques that defined Creole cuisine, yet she was unafraid to adopt new technologies, materials, and business practices. This adaptability ensured that her offerings remained relevant in a changing market. By integrating innovation with respect for culinary roots, she created products that honored tradition while satisfying contemporary demands—a delicate balance few restaurateurs or entrepreneurs achieve.

Financial management and strategic foresight were essential throughout her entrepreneurial ventures. Lena kept meticulous records of ingredient costs, labor, and overhead, using these metrics to inform pricing, menu adjustments, and investment in equipment. Her ability to forecast demand, manage production schedules, and optimize workflow ensured profitability while maintaining high quality. These skills underscored that entrepreneurship was not simply about culinary talent; it required strategic planning, disciplined execution, and a willingness to adapt to evolving markets.

Mentorship and staff development remained a critical component of her business model. Lena trained employees to understand not just recipes but operational principles: portion control, sanitation, client relations, and quality assurance. Staff who learned under her guidance became proficient in both culinary technique and business operations, amplifying the reach and impact of her ventures. By investing in people as well as products, Lena created an ecosystem that sustained her businesses and ensured continuity even as demand increased.

Her entrepreneurial vision also included public engagement. Lena's media presence, cookbooks, and cooking demonstrations served as platforms to promote her catering and frozen food products. She understood that consumers responded to personality, credibility, and visibility. By integrating media exposure with business strategy, she created a multi-channel approach that expanded reach and reinforced brand identity. Each new venture—from radio demonstrations to frozen meals—benefited from the credibility she had established over decades.

Through catering and frozen food production, Lena Richard redefined what it meant to be a chef-entrepreneur in mid-twentieth-century America. She demonstrated that culinary skill could be translated into scalable business opportunities without sacrificing quality, cultural authenticity, or personal vision. Her efforts challenged conventional limitations imposed by race, gender, and geography, illustrating that innovation, strategy, and mastery of craft could create enduring economic and cultural impact.

The ripple effect of her entrepreneurial ventures was profound. Not only did her products reach homes and events beyond New Orleans, but her example inspired other chefs and businesspeople to pursue similar paths. She modeled a comprehensive approach to food entrepreneurship: skillful execution, operational discipline, strategic marketing, and brand development—all anchored by deep cultural knowledge. Her career proved that culinary entrepreneurship could be a vehicle for empowerment, cultural preservation, and lasting influence, making her a pioneer whose lessons continue to resonate across generations.

By combining catering, frozen foods, media exposure, and education, Lena Richard created an interconnected network of enterprises that amplified her impact. Each plate served, each package shipped, and each student trained contributed to a larger vision: a sustainable, respected, and widely recognized Creole culinary brand. Her approach demonstrated that food is more than a profession—it is a platform for entrepreneurship, cultural leadership, and societal influence, and Lena Richard mastered all three with unparalleled skill and foresight.

# Chapter ten

# A Legacy That Still Feeds the Soul

Lena Richard's legacy is a feast that continues to nourish hearts, minds, and taste buds long after her own kitchen lights dimmed. Her life's work—spanning restaurants, catering, media appearances, cookbooks, and culinary education—was never solely about food. It was about culture, innovation, empowerment, and leaving a blueprint for others to follow. Every dish she prepared, every student she trained, and every recipe she shared was a thread in a tapestry that wove together the richness of Creole heritage, the discipline of professional cooking, and the audacity of entrepreneurship.

One of the most enduring aspects of Lena Richard's impact is her preservation of Creole culinary tradition. Through her meticulous cookbooks, she captured not just recipes but techniques, timing, and flavor philosophies that might otherwise have been lost in private kitchens. Her instructions were clear, precise, and accessible, ensuring that generations of home cooks and professional chefs could replicate her dishes without losing authenticity. From delicate pastries to robust gumbo, Richard codified Creole cooking in a way that respected its roots while making it reproducible—a crucial step in transforming regional cuisine into a national culinary treasure.

Her educational work amplified this legacy. Students who passed through her classrooms carried forward both her methods and her standards. She taught more than the mechanics of cooking; she instilled values of discipline, precision, and pride in cultural heritage. These students went on to open their own kitchens, teach their own classes, and inspire new chefs, creating a ripple effect that extended far beyond New Orleans. Lena's vision was not limited to individual success; she sought to cultivate a network of culinary practitioners who could elevate Creole cuisine on every stage—home, restaurant, and classroom alike.

Media played a crucial role in making Lena's influence national and even international. Her radio shows and television appearances brought the sights, sounds, and stories of New Orleans kitchens into living rooms across the country. Listeners and viewers were not merely learning recipes—they were experiencing a culture. Lena's calm authority, warmth, and meticulous demonstrations invited audiences into a world that was at once professional and intimate, sophisticated yet approachable. By mastering the art of communication, she ensured that her culinary philosophy reached far beyond those who could physically enter her kitchen.

Entrepreneurship was another key pillar of her lasting impact. Lena demonstrated that a chef's work could be transformed into a viable business, encompassing restaurants, catering, frozen foods, and media ventures. She showed how creativity, discipline, and strategic thinking could be leveraged to create scalable enterprises. Her career offered a model for future generations, particularly women and people of color, proving that success in the culinary arts required not just talent but vision, planning, and resilience. She turned the art of cooking into a platform for empowerment and professional legitimacy.

Cultural advocacy was inseparable from her work. In an era of segregation and limited opportunity for Black professionals, Lena's prominence challenged societal norms. Every dish she prepared, every public appearance she made, and every student she mentored was a subtle but powerful assertion of capability, excellence, and leadership. She demonstrated that Creole cuisine was not merely comfort food—it was sophisticated, complex, and deserving of respect. Her success carved a space for Black women in culinary media and professional kitchens, breaking barriers that many believed were unbreachable.

Lena's cookbooks remain central to her enduring influence. They are more than collections of recipes; they are instructional guides, historical records, and cultural documents. For contemporary chefs, historians, and home cooks, her work offers insight into both the techniques and the social contexts of early twentieth-century Creole cooking. Recipes that might once have existed only in the memory of family cooks were now accessible to a national audience. The clarity and precision with which she recorded methods ensured that her approach to cooking could be learned, replicated, and adapted by anyone willing to follow her guidance.

Her legacy also persists in the broader culinary imagination. Today, chefs, culinary schools, and food historians often reference Lena Richard as a pioneer who bridged tradition and modernity, artistry and business, culture and commerce. Her life demonstrates that cooking can be a means of expression, a form of cultural preservation, and a vehicle for entrepreneurship—all simultaneously. By integrating these dimensions, she set a precedent for how chefs could navigate multiple roles while staying true to their craft and heritage.

Family and intergenerational connections were also vital to Lena's influence. She often collaborated with her daughter, students, and staff in producing her cookbooks and managing her enterprises. This collaborative approach extended the reach of her expertise while fostering mentorship, continuity, and shared learning. Her method of passing knowledge—through direct instruction, demonstration, and documentation—ensured that her culinary philosophy survived beyond her own lifetime, embedded in the practices of those who learned directly from her or from her written work.

Perhaps most importantly, Lena Richard's legacy continues to "feed the soul" in a literal and figurative sense. Her recipes provide nourishment, yes, but they also offer a taste of history, a connection to New Orleans, and a sense of belonging in a culinary lineage that values both precision and creativity. For home cooks, her instructions create moments of discovery and accomplishment. For professional chefs, her work exemplifies standards of excellence and dedication to craft. And for communities, her career represents possibility, resilience, and the enduring impact of cultural stewardship.

Even decades after her passing, Lena Richard's influence reverberates in classrooms, kitchens, and dining rooms. Her teaching philosophy—emphasizing discipline, creativity, and cultural pride—remains relevant to aspiring chefs. Her media presence continues to inspire culinary storytelling and demonstrates how chefs can connect with audiences beyond the plate. Her entrepreneurial achievements offer a blueprint for turning culinary expertise into sustainable, scalable ventures. And her cookbooks stand as timeless records of technique, flavor, and tradition.

Through all of these avenues, Lena Richard's work remains alive, dynamic, and instructive. She transformed Creole cooking from a regional specialty into a nationally recognized art form, ensuring that both the craft and the culture behind it would be respected, studied, and celebrated for generations. Every dish prepared from her recipes, every student trained under her guidance, and every chef influenced by her pioneering spirit carries forward a piece of her vision.

Ultimately, Lena Richard's legacy is a testament to what happens when talent meets vision, when cultural pride meets entrepreneurial strategy, and when mastery of craft meets the courage to break barriers. It is a legacy that nourishes not just bodies, but minds and spirits—a living, breathing testament to the power of food, education, and determination. Through her work, generations continue to experience the richness of Creole cuisine, the value of disciplined practice, and the inspiration of a trailblazer who refused to let societal limitations define her.

Thank you, dear reader, for dedicating your valuable time, attention, and curiosity to journey through the life and legacy of Lena Richard. Your decision to open these pages, to immerse yourself in her story, and to reflect on her triumphs and challenges is what gives this book its very purpose. Without your engagement, without your willingness to witness the struggles, the brilliance, and the relentless drive of a woman who reshaped Creole cuisine and the culinary world, this biography would be nothing more than ink on paper. It is your eyes that bring her kitchen to life, your imagination that fills in the aromas, the textures, and the heartbeat of New Orleans that Lena so lovingly preserved and shared.

By reading this book, you have not just learned about recipes or restaurant management—you have connected with history, culture, and the indomitable spirit of a trailblazer who turned every challenge into an opportunity. Lena Richard's story is a reminder of what is possible when passion meets determination, when talent is paired with vision, and when resilience defies societal limitations. Your choice to invest in this journey is a testament to your own curiosity, your appreciation for heritage, and your respect for pioneers who have paved the way for others to flourish.

If this biography has inspired you, if Lena's story has awakened a spark of creativity, ambition, or admiration in your heart, I humbly ask for your support. A positive review from you does more than just help this book—it ensures that Lena Richard's story reaches others who need inspiration, who need to see that barriers can be broken and dreams can be realized. Every thoughtful review amplifies her voice, preserves her legacy, and allows future readers to connect with her life, her work, and her enduring impact.

This book is not just a chronicle; it is an invitation. An invitation to honor perseverance, to celebrate cultural ingenuity, and to recognize the extraordinary achievements of a woman whose influence continues to feed, educate, and inspire countless generations. It is a perfect gift for those who cherish culinary history, for young minds eager to learn about resilience and creativity, and for adults who appreciate stories of courage, entrepreneurship, and cultural pride.

So, dear reader, let your engagement continue beyond these pages. Share Lena Richard's story, let it inspire conversations, and consider leaving your mark with a review that helps others discover her remarkable journey. Your support ensures that her legacy not only lives on but grows stronger with each reader who steps into her world. Thank you for being a vital part of this story—because without you, Lena's kitchen, her classrooms, her books, and her vision would never fully reach the audience they were meant to touch.

Printed in Dunstable, United Kingdom